THE GRIEVING TIME

A Month by Month Account of Recovery from Loss

By Anne M. Brooks

Illustrated by Ted Ramsey

DELAPEAKE
PUBLISHING COMPANY
WILMINGTON, DELAWARE 19899

Copyright © 1982 by Anne M. Brooks

Printed in the United States of America

Library of Congress Card Number 82-17955

ISBN: 0-911293-00-0

PREFACE

THE GRIEVING TIME was written as a once a month journal for the first half of the year following my husband's death of cancer at 61. The writing is spontaneous, emotional and purposefully unedited. Beginning the journal as an answer to my need, I grew to realize its value as a therapeutic tool. Everytime I wrote or reread it, there was a comfort of releasing sublimated grief.

Nowhere in book stores or libraries could I find any other such help. Sentimental poetry, clinical aids, religious tracts, rather long autobiographies, yes, but nothing that moved me to that needed comfort.

I hope that readers, too, will feel that the depth of their personal grief is real, it is honest, and they are not alone.

The first few days I feel as though I am sitting in a tree somewhere, watching myself perform. I try to do all the right things —the greetings to relatives, the thank-yous, the speech at the service, more thank-yous, more smiles, more greetings. I am outside myself —as if I have switched off my feelings.

Except that suddenly right in the middle of a conversation, a wave of reality washes over me and I have to leave, quickly, to hide somewhere. I have to hold on to something when it happens — a pillow, the refrigerator, one of his shirts — because of the terrible pain in my chest. Is it my heart? If I think of him, I have genuine waves of feeling sick as well as the pain.

At first I try not to think of him; it hurts too much. Then as the days go by that's all I do but it's thinking only of the long illness and especially the terrible last three weeks. I think of the special things he said, "What would I do without you?" "Let me feel your hair."

I am so glad I insisted someone sit with him every minute the last two weeks. Every time he opened his eyes, he would look to see if we were there beside him, and we were. He let us hold his hand all night. There was so much love in the room he must have been comforted.

I hope, oh so much, that although he was unconscious, that somehow he knew when I crawled into bed with him and lay alone with him in my arms as he died.

So much love he took with him.

After all the family leaves, the silence is overwhelming. I try not to think, keep frantically busy — lawyers, the bank, letters to write all day.

The best, the only good time of all twenty-four hours is when I first get into my single bed at night — I have

never gone back to the big bed. I am dead, bone-aching tired, but just as I turn over on my side and start to cry quietly, clutching his blue denim shirt in a ball to me, a slow, warm, comforting feeling comes over me. A presence so loving, so comforting. Is it him? It must be.

THE SECOND MONTH

Why can't I dream of him? It is the second month and I can simply not visualize his face or form. I stare at his picture and can feel my hand on his cheek, or smoothing down hair, but as soon as I put down the picture, he's gone. I try and try. I long to see him, but I dare not look at snapshots or home movies. I will be torn apart.

I would never have believed the physical side of grief. I do feel torn apart. Does this come first, or after the numbness which is its other half of each day? There seems to be nothing in between.

That's not altogether true. A little while each day, I seem to be functioning, mechanically, but still it is a semblance of living. No, not living, existing.

I don't like anything. Not food, not friends, not music.

I love the children, the grown-up ones and the grandchildren. They are my only comfort. They all try so hard to help me, but I am in a world apart even from them. I am surprised at the depth of their feelings, their own grief. They cannot possibly feel as badly as I do; their grief is different. I am wrapped in self-absorption, denying it is self pity. I find faults in all my friends. Why did I ever like them?

Something must be done. I will not be a whining, self-pitying widow. I go to the library and check out every book on grief and widowhood. I finally read all the pamphlets my daughter has sent.

I realize that part of my problem is I cannot really share any of my feeling with anyone unless I feel they have recently gone through the same experience. So I bridge social chasms and call up one woman whose husband is dying and another whose husband has just died. I don't even know them, but I stumble through an explanation — maybe I can help them while they help me.

We do meet, and talk, and it is a help to me. I feel useful, besides. This is a good move. I'll do it again.

I have lost twelve pounds and everyone notices. It's not only because I'm not liking food, it's my frenetic activity and sleepless nights. I'll sleep well a few nights and then two in a row I'll lie there hour after hour, hating my life, wishing I could turn the clock back.

I have not gone through all the states mentioned in the books and pamphlets. I've never felt guilty, because all our lives we knew we had the best there was, and we tried to appreciate every moment. Then, too, I tried so hard to give him everything I had these last two years. The way he died, too, in my arms —no guilt there. It was the way it should be.

Not even anger. Having been so close the whole time, the end seemed inevitable. Inexorable. At the very end, he wanted "out" so much, I could not dream of trying to keep him.

I am finally dreaming of him! It is such a comfort, so natural. At first, he was only a shadowy figure, a presence, but now he is there!

The practical aspects of living creep up on me. All the business affairs take up time and I prefer them — nothing personal to cope with.

The social part of my life is exactly what the books and articles say. Many old friends have disappeared into the woodwork. Never call, never invite me, seem embarrassed when we meet. I make special efforts to talk about him naturally, to ease their embarrassment. Some doors have just shut, I guess, so I'll have to find others.

But some friends remain — I appreciate their every gesture. New friends who never knew him appear and I am pleased to be accepted. Maybe I am a person without him, although I only feel like a half.

Large parties are deadly. He isn't there for the entrance or leave-taking. I no longer have him to gravitate toward

when I'm bored or feeling uncertain. I know these feelings are not so important: they will ease with time.

People keep saying, "It all will get better." The strange thing is I'm not sure I want it to. My grief, the terrible longings, all the agony, are what seem to hold me still close to him. When I cry or rock myself in misery, I feel him near and even call his name.

I am completely asexual (another thing the books say), but there are strange sensual reactions. I hate to take a shower — I am reminded so much how much he loved me. I look at my hands or even my feet and think those are the hands and feet he loved so much. My clothes are all associated with him. I hate them.

The longing to be held, to put my cheek against his, to dance with him is unbearable. I dance one afternoon by myself in the kitchen, tears streaming down my face as the radio plays swing music.

Whatever shall I do?

THE FOURTH MONTH

I'm fine.

People keep asking, I keep answering, I'm fine. I'm fine.

I smile. I walk briskly. I manage the business affairs extremely well. I go to the few parties to which I'm invited. I smile. I even laugh. I'm fine.

And then when I drive over the bay bridge I don't dare take my eyes off the pavement or I'll see a sailboat, or even just white caps, and I'll burst into tears. But only if I'm alone.

That's the key word. Alone. Dreading it, avoiding it, but needing it. Needing time to be alone to grieve, to cry. And I really mean to cry — loudly, when no one can hear me. Except him, I hope. Time alone when I lean my head against the back door window and cry because the sunset is so beautiful and I almost called, "Come see how beautiful it is!" to someone who isn't there.

Time to be alone, to learn to steel myself to the idea of years ahead. Not just the days I'm barely able to manage, nor the months I dread, but maybe years. Years of no sharing thoughts, or dreams, nor any beautiful things, no special moments, no joy.

Years of looking at the house and the things in the house, every single thing in it meaning something about him. He bought it. He fixed it. He painted it. He made it. We found it. Nowhere can I look but what he's there. I can't put a log on the fire without seeing him kneel on one knee and do the same.

I can't bear to go in the bedroom where we spent all the nights of loving. All the mornings of lying curled together as though we would never part.

I never dreamed we would. Even the months he was so sick, I kept denying the reality. I kept feeling it was a bad dream. Of course, he'd get better. Of course, he'd never go.

I'm suddenly angry now. Angry that any of it happened. He tried so hard to get better. We fought together. Nights before we went to sleep, we always touched each other's hand. Lots of times we even said the words, "We'll fight it."

And the first one awake in the morning slid over to the other right away. We'd hold on for dear life — so glad we were both still curled up together.

They say it is only the possibility of committing suicide that keeps grief-stricken people from going mad. It's absolutely true. In the moments of terrible total despair, there has to be an alternative to those awful words that haunt —

Forever
Never again
Alone
I'm fine.

I feel as though I am acting in a play and suddenly, at the beginning of the last act, someone has changed the script. I hate the play now ... although I loved it before; but I have to keep on playing my part although it is all wrong for me. I have to think of the rest of the cast and the audience, but I long for the curtain to fall ... to free me from the acting.

People look at me so warily. Is she going to cry if we mention his name? So of course they never do. I, and the children, are the only ones who do. It is easier to do now, but easier doesn't mean easy.

There is no question in my mind that the degree of grief one feels is in direct proportion to the depth of feeling one had before the loss. Everyone feels the separation, some more than others. Some feel anger, some guilt, some fear, some frustration.

But real grief, the kind that shakes your whole being and feels as though you cannot possibly bear it, that is grief, not just loss.

I remember parts of old hymns: "Oh love that will not let me go" — "Remember me." These bits and pieces are the only solace I have found in religion. I don't really believe in heaven, but I do believe he is somewhere. That belief is the thin thread that holds my sanity, the thought that perhaps,

someday, somehow, I will be with him again. This is half the magnetism drawing me to suicide; the other half is simply that life is too unbearable without him.

I have come a long way in five months. For so long, the thought of suicide was lurking behind every move. The promises I had given him deterred me more than anything. Then came emergencies; I really was needed with the new baby, with other problems. I think of what he said to me when we talked about it, "Think of what it would do to the children." Now suicide is relegated to the future; it is my alternative, not my consuming desire.

When the children and grandchildren are around, I realize how far I have come; I come alive. I can talk about him, think about him, laugh about memories with them, all without pain. I still cannot do this when I'm alone.

The spaces of coping and not coping have finally reversed. Most of the time I really am not fine, but not so bad. The good days are more frequent than the difficult ones now, although the pain, when it comes, is still as intense.

Perhaps all the positive moves I made have paid off; the reaching out to other *widows, all the reading, the talking to the children. I have forced myself to express my thoughts. Some sort of creative activity, painting, photography, sewing, knitting — anything that makes me feel that I have passed the time productively —is therapeutic. I think I have reached this point faster than many other grievers because I have tried so hard. I listened to every suggestion, accepted every invitation. I had to, or I never could have survived.*

Having some of the children so close, with one daughter staying with me for awhile, has helped more than anything else. Just to feel their arms around me on a particularly bad day saves me. They encourage me in all my ventures, support my every move. I feel like their child, but I need this so much.

I think I will have to buy a dog. I must have something near me I can love, that I can touch, can hug.

I am not yet whole. I never will be whole again; but I guess I will be me.

THE SIXTH MONTH

POSTSCRIPT

This is a testament to love and loss.
To withhold grief is destructive;
to release it, healing.
The writing of this book was my life-line.
May the reading help your grieving time.
You are not alone.